Alchemy

Ethical
Muslim Stories

Muslims' Internal Conversations

for Everyone Who Values the Deeper Meanings

[Teenage Audience Adaptation]

Medina House Publishing

Cover Design: Medina House Publishing

Medina House
publishing

www.medinahouse.org
170 Manhattan Ave PO Box 63
Buffalo, New York 14215
contact@medinahouse.org

Published in the United States of America.

DEDICATION

Dedicated to all young adults in search of the truth.

Contents

Contents

Contents

Contents

Contents

Contents

ACKNOWLEDGMENTS

Many thanks to Dr. Yunus Kumek for granting us the
permission to adapt the original stories for a teenage audience

1. Hear the Crickets

A red ant made the life changing decision to embark on pilgrimage. Its friend, the Cricket, advised it against what it believed to be a foolish decision. The following conversation ensued between them:

The Cricket: I don't think you will make it. The holy sites are several thousands of miles away from our current location.

The Ant: You might be right.

The Cricket: Then why are you going?

The Ant: I only focus on the part that matters.

The Cricket fell silent, lowered its head and reflected on the words of Allah's Messenger ﷺ: "Verily actions are judged by intentions."

In practice…

According to prophetic traditions, intentions precede actions. If our intent is for the good and beneficial, Allah سبحانه وتعالى rewards us accordingly. If a person prays or gives charity to the poor with the intention of showing off to people or to gain some worldly benefit, then the person can get what he (she) desires in the world. After death, he (she) may be punished due to insincere actions.

2. Stay Grounded

There was a poor Muslim in the mosque. He bought a small coffee machine and placed it in the mosque. While staying in the mosque, he would serve people of the community. As time passed, the people began to respect him because he was so generous and considerate. The man gained a reputation as the "most selfless person in the mosque." Our poor friend was now in dangerous territory.

In practice…

Power, responsibility and positions bring recognition. This can bring about feelings of arrogance which can destroy the rewards of the spiritual aspirant. If one desires to be recognized by Allah سبحانه وتعالى , then he (she) should imbibe humbleness and appreciation of the Divine.

3. Spirituality and Service

Bilal owned a coffee spot downtown that was quite famous in his area. At his local mosque's classes, people constantly requested for samples of his rare imported beans and tips on how to make the perfect cup. Bilal began to get upset and felt that his spiritual progress was stunted by the constant interruptions. He felt the need for people to acknowledge him for more than his coffee brewing skills. This agitation increased until a Friday sermon on humility brought Bilal back to reality. At the end of the prayers, he set up a table in the masjid parking lot and began giving out free samples of his best brews. Internally, he prayed for spiritual elevation.

In practice...

If we try to hold our egos tightly, the disturbances will increase. Therefore, one should let it go in order to taste the pleasure and satisfaction of serving others. This, alongside worship, is a means to spiritual growth.

4. Test or Treat

One afternoon, Adnan was reading and memorizing the Quran. He spent a good amount of time with the sacred Book. Then, he took a tea break. As soon as he got near the kettle, he saw his favorite cookie miraculously appear next to the coffee machine. He said to himself, "There is no one in the mosque except me. Who brought this cookie? I know this cookie is not local". Adnan asked Allah سبحانه وتعالى for forgiveness, took his cup of tea and left the cookie where he found it.

In practice...

Sometimes, in spiritual practice, miracles or supernatural occurrences are metaphorized as cookies. Cookies may come in different forms as one engages in practices such as reading (or memorizing) the Quran, praying, fasting, etc. The real question is: Is the cookie healthy? In essence, is it an encouragement by God on the path?, Is it a test or trial from God to see if the person on the path will be arrogant by claiming supernatural incidents and try to be superior to their fellow Muslims?

5. Ali Argues with His Wife

One day, Ali was in an argument with his wife. After the episode, he decided to discuss some of their marital issues:

Ali: I need to tell you something.

His wife: You are probably going to remind me about everything I did wrong this week!

Ali: You already told your parents about all my faults, so I was just following suit.

His Wife: You claim to be a Muslim and you are worried about what people think about you. Shame on you!

Ali: Do you think we are monks? Please, stop being naive.

After the argument was over, Ali was overcome by a strong feeling of remorse in his heart. He approached his wife again to speak.

Ali: I appreciate you; I love you and I am so sorry.

The argument was over. Ali said, "*Alhamdulillah* for the teachings of the Prophet Muhammad ﷺ. We emulate manhood from the best of men.

In practice…

In healthy marital relationships, the wife is always right. The husband's expected demeanor is to always maintain silence and remain passive in any dispute. The high road is to forgive and move on.

6. The Best Voice

There was a man in the local mosque who had a beautiful voice that he used to call people to prayer[1]. As soon as he starts the call to prayer, the people in the mosque would begin to weep due to his melodious recitation. As the man began to take notice, he began to exaggerate his recitation, trying to further gain the attention and admiration of the congregation. His attempts were very distasteful, and the people began to dislike it. One day after the *Fajr* prayer, his close friend invited him out for breakfast at the local pancake spot. The intent was to use the sweetness of the pancake syrup to offset the bitter truth he was about to tell his friend.

In practice...

Sometimes, the spiritual disease(s) can become the character(s) of a person if there are no friends to help identify one's mistakes and shortcomings. Ostentation or "showing-off" is a major spiritual disease. Therefore, it is a good practice to keep company of those who are willing to tell you your mistakes rather than those that simply praise your achievements. One sage says, "I love a friend who warns me about a scorpion on my chest. Why should I get angry with him?"

---

[1] *Adhan:* The Muslim call to prayer.

7. Looking in the Mirror

Hamza did not like to look in the mirror. Hence, he was unaware of his appearance. His messy hair, untrimmed moustache, uncombed beard, and un-ironed shirts all went unnoticed to him, until his friend, Jaafar, approached him and brought the issue to his attention.

In practice…

Similarly, our internal "messiness" is ugly. Allah سبحانه وتعالى created everyone with some degree of internal beauty as well as some level of physical beauty. Arrogance, hatred, anger, and jealousy are the essence of ugliness. If the person does not have "mirrors" to reflect on those, then that is the real problem. The Prophet Muhammad ﷺ is reported to have said, "The believer is the mirror of the believer."

8. Value of A Book

Zahid was a righteous man, yet he was known to live from "paycheck to paycheck". One day, one of the wealthier congregants was showing off a rare book of prophetic supplications. Zahid saw this book and approached him.

Zahid: Can I buy this book from you?

The man smiled sarcastically at Zahid and said: "I know that you have little money. How can you pay for this book?"

The seeker of knowledge reached deep into his pocket and took out fresh bills he had received from his most recent job and handed the entire fistful to the man without thinking.

The man was shocked and said, "Here is the book. It is a gift from me. I don't want the money."

In practice…

From this story, we can understand that the market value of the book was known to be quite substantial. However, the poor man was willing to trade all his money for the book. The book was full of prayers from the best of mankind, Prophet Muhammad ﷺ. In Islam, anything valuable in the relationship with God has a very high price. Muslims don't assign inherent worth on anything related to this mundane world, but they rather place high premiums on those that are connected to the Divine.

9. Ask the Right One

Wakeel was sitting in the masjid and revising some verses of the Noble Quran. With a solemn demeanor, one of the masjid youths approached him. Wakeel concluded his devotion and engaged the young man in a discussion. The adolescent expressed his dissatisfaction with the injustices, evils and sufferings existing in the world. He also indicated his helplessness in providing a viable solution to address such issues. Wakeel further engaged him in a discussion:

Wakeel: Did you express your worries to Allah سبحانه وتعالى؟

The youth did not respond but seemed displeased with Wakeel's question. Perceiving this, Wakeel continued: Look! I understand you want to do something. Right?

The youth: Yes.

Wakeel: How do you do it? You have ideas and then you put them into action, right?

The youth: Right.

Wakeel: So, ask Allah سبحانه وتعالى to inspire you with the right and relevant ideas about what you want to do. Then, leave the results to the only One who can control them.

In practice…

In Islam, relying on Allah سبحانه وتعالى for guidance is very important. One can ask God to make it easy in choosing the right choice in any decision-making process. Islam encourages and expects a constant dialogue between the Divine and humans.

10.   Divine Gifts

There was a peculiar older man named Kashfy who used to frequently attend the congregational prayers. He often sits in the front row of the mosque for a few minutes before and after each prayer. One sunny day as one of the congregants was leaving the masjid, Kashfy attempted to give him an umbrella as a gift before the young man stepped out into the parking lot. The young man rejected the offer with a rude gesture of his left hand, without even speaking to Kashfy. He then proceeded to his car, murmuring to himself about how strange the elders at the masjid were. Kashfy went back to his regular spot in the masjid and sat down to remember Allah سبحانه وتعالى. Suddenly, rain splatters could be heard pounding the masjid roof and windows. Kashfy began to laugh aloud.

In practice…

It is quite possible for a human being who constantly engages in Divine remembrance to be gifted with stronger instincts than your average person. The Messenger of Allah ﷺ, peace be upon him, said, "Beware of the intuition of the believer. Verily, he sees with the light of Allah." Although, "normal people" can think that these people are weird, their unique nature is closer to the natural human disposition.

11.   Blinded by the Closeness

Everyone in the community eagerly looked forward to the weekly Friday sermons in the local mosque. The resident imam was well known for his erudition and his ability to attract huge crowds. In fact, to sit in his discourse was indeed a priceless gift. Each Friday, every member of the congregation could be seen listening attentively to the respected imam. That is, every member of the congregation except for one. In attendance each week was a teenage boy who could be seen sitting in the same spot, wearing the same cap and fidgeting with his mobile phone. One Friday, a bewildered visitor enquired about the identity of this rude teenager. In response, one of the local community members chuckled as he sighed: "That is the Imam's son!"

In practice…

There are people who work in the masjids. They may be externally close to religious activities and personalities, but they are easily distracted and very far away from Allah سبحانه وتعالى. Sometimes, the closeness can make a person blind and have an undesirable effect. Similarly, some Muslim theologians assert that Allah سبحانه وتعالى is so obvious that if people cannot acknowledge Allah سبحانه وتعالى, then it is due to this kind of blindness. Signs of Allah سبحانه through His creations abound in all spheres of life.

13

12. Homecoming

There was an announcement in the mosque detailing the information related to the funeral prayer for Brother Abdullah who had recently passed." After discussing the matter for a few minutes, one of the elders named Hakeem was asked if he was going home. He replied: "No. Brother Abdullah is going home."

In practice…

For the righteous, death is the joyful moment of meeting with Allah سبحانه وتعالى . If the person is eager to meet with Allah سبحانه وتعالى, then Allah سبحانه وتعالى also wants to meet with him (her). In the teachings of the Prophet Muhammad ﷺ , it said that Allah سبحانه وتعالى will treat the person in the way that he(she) expects to be treated in the afterlife.

13.   Practice What You Preach

The masjid's weekly evening classes were dedicated to teaching the community members about different virtues and how to inculcate them. For one week in each month, a different guest Imam will be invited to educate the small study circle on a new character trait. One week, a guest Imam sat down at the beginning of the class and began to distribute tea and snacks to all the people present. This continued for a full 15 minutes before one of the elders became irritated and demanded to know the topic of the evening class. In amusement and with a grin on his face, the guest Imam paused and replied, "Patience is our topic for this evening".

In practice…

Rather than just incessant preaching, the best way of teaching a virtue is through actual experience. Islam also teaches that the best ways to inculcate a virtue is to keep company of those blessed with such a virtue.

14.   Scents Affect Your Sense

A group of men entered a class on the Prophet Muhammad's ﷺ character. As they formed a circle and awaited commencement of the class, their teacher placed some incense in a decorated vase and set the wood shavings alight. He then encouraged the students to pass the vase from one person to another, allowing the fragrant smoke to cover their clothing. "What is this?", yelled a particularly impatient young man, questioning the purpose of the practice. "It is a study aid", replied their teacher calmly.

In practice…

Prophetic teachings state that bad smell or bad actions will repel angels and make any type of spiritual inspirations unlikely. In this story, the teacher used the incense as a practical means to impact the nature of the spiritual gathering.

15. Washroom Whispers

Prior to his interview, Yusha found himself plagued with a fear of failure and doubt in his own abilities. In a bid to mentally prepare himself, he paced back and forth in the restroom. Thereafter, Yunus entered the restroom to find his friend next to the stall and asked what his issue was.

"I am trying to get my mind right," replied Yusha.

"And you picked the worst possible place to do it," replied Yunus.

In practice…

In the Islamic tradition, the bathroom is understood to be home to devils and other unseen creatures that induce whispers and insinuations in the minds of humans. Hence, one is advised to spend minimal time in the bathroom.

16. Elevator Issues

The elevator stopped in between the floors. Everyone was complaining and frantically pushing the buttons, but the elevator wouldn't budge. Tamer was smiling, waiting for the people to calm down. Finally, he stepped forward and said: *"Bismillah* – In the name of God", and then pressed the ground floor button. Alas, the elevator started moving towards the ground floor.

In practice…

According to Islamic theology, the outward worldly mechanisms are merely a means through which the Divine action takes place. Muslims believe that the Creator does not need these means to implement His will but permits their creation (or invention) in order to test humans.

17. Embrace Meaning

Arif used to compose bedtime stories for his children each night. He would encourage his kids' contributions in these stories. Together, they would constantly alternate the backgrounds of the stories, switching from old-western settings to futuristic sci-fi plots. However, regardless of the narrative, they would always ensure they incorporated good morals and values in the stories.

After each composition, Arif would supplicate: "May Allah grant us the ability to see reality for what it is".

In practice…

In the Quran and other prophetic teachings, various parables and different stories from different time periods are presented in order to convey certain timeless principles. It is important to be able to absorb the core teachings from these anecdotes without being distracted by names, times or places or plots.

18.   From Service to Worship

In the last few nights of Ramadan, the mosque generally stayed packed with people praying, reciting the Quran and making supplications to their Lord. The entire masjid would buzz with the sound of the remembrance of Allah سبحانه وتعالى. During the hour prior to sunset, a group of children were assigned to prepare the area in the mosque where the congregants break their fast. One day, as one group of boys were setting up the tablecloth on the floor, two little girls ran across the area and threw dates all around. Pitchers of juices were also carefully placed in the center with stacks of plastic cups placed next to one another. Their parents smiled as they watched the children and one father remarked: "They will *inshaAllah* become great worshippers."

In practice…

In Muslim cultures, the concept of service is very prominent in social and familial relationship. This is used as a way of training children and tempering their egos through service to humanity and nature. This, in turn serves as a veritable foothold in the service of the Creator.

19.   Spoiling A Sweet Brew

One day, Zahir made a sizzling fresh pot of coffee in the morning. He was sipping the nice, fresh brew and enjoying enormous pleasure from every sip. Then, his son, Safwan turned a corner of the kitchen and ran straight into his father. Thus, Zahir spilled the coffee on himself and immediately jumped up from the heat of the scalding liquid.

"What is wrong with you?", screamed Zahir, leading his son to scurry off with tears in his eyes. Zahir proceeded to take another sip of his coffee, but it did not taste as good anymore.

In practice…

In attaining spiritual pleasure, a slight hint of arrogance can nullify all the efforts expended on the journey. The Prophet says, "A person who has an atom's size of arrogance in his (her) heart will not enter paradise and smell the fragrance of it." The antidotes to arrogance in the journey are modesty and humility. One can achieve these by constantly prostrating and bowing before God and glorifying Him. Also, any thoughts or feelings of arrogance should be immediately addressed. Otherwise, the disease can grow uncontrollably like a cancerous cell.

20.   Emptying Out

Fatimah was about to begin her salah. As she extended her right hand down her jacket pocket, she felt candy wraps, notes, beads, a napkin, some coins, and other items. When she raised her hand for the opening of the prayer, she heard the jingle of the items in her pocket. So, she took off this jacket and prayed wearing one with empty pockets. She knew deep inside her heart that her decision was the only way her prayers would have its desired effect.

In practice…

The practice of detachment from the mundane world during the prayers (and chants) is very important. One cannot fully practice spiritual emptying or discharge if mindful detachment is not present. According to some of the scholars, raising one's hands back and forth between each bodily movement during salah is the mental reminder of disgust and detachment from all worldly engagements.

21. Sweet Motivation

Each day, Mohamoud would attend the mosque for the evening prayer. At the end of the prayer, he would reach into his pocket for a bag of sweets. He would then distribute the candies to each child that accompanied his(her) parent(s) to the mosque. As the kids thanked him enthusiastically, he will gently remind them that if they maintain the beautiful tradition of prayer, the real Giver will honor them with a gift that is much sweeter than candy.

In practice...

Mohamoud used the candy as an incentive to motivate the children. Similarly, when we decide to take our religious life more seriously, we may receive gifts in the form of worldly blessings, but these gifts are just resources to drive us towards the main goal, which is the pleasure of Allah سبحانه وتعالى.

22. Conceal Your Gifts

Pasha spent most of his free time reciting the Quran in the local mosque. This practice made his voice beautiful and his recitation melodious. One day, as he recited, another young man came in and began to listen closely to Pasha's recitations. Immediately, Pasha began to lower his voice and he eventually stopped altogether. The young man thought Pasha was tired and proceeded to leave the mosque. As soon as the young man left the praying hall, Pasha smiled and resumed his recitation from where he left off.

In practice…

It is a very common historical occurrence that the actions or jealousy of people often puts the righteous in jeopardy. Therefore, some of the pious have adopted the habit of using their humanity to disguise their religiosity.

23.   Travel to the Divine

Yunus's wife, Samirah, had not seen her brother in a very long time. Hence, Yunus suggested that they pay him a visit.

Yunus: Why don't we visit your brother?

Samirah: What a great idea! Let's go!

Yunus: Do you want your sister to come along too?

Samirah: Absolutely!

Samirah: How about your mom? Why don't you take her too?

Samirah: Thank you, honey! You are so thoughtful.

A day later....

Yunus: Honey, I would love to accompany you on the trip, but I wouldn't want to intrude in your re-union. You can go with your family and reminisce about the old times.

Samirah: That is so sweet! Are you sure? You don't want to come with us?

Yunus: Not this time.

Samirah: Okay.

Yunus's prayer beads jingled in his pocket as he walked away.

In practice...

Deeply spiritual people always prefer spending time with Allah

سبحانه وتعالى . They are very jealous about their relationship with Allah

سبحانه وتعالى . Any engagement should be really something worthy or else it's not worth sacrificing these sweet moments of spending time with the Creator in worship. In the story, Yunus found an excuse not to accompany his wife so he could engage in more worship.

24. Intention Check

Yunus's wife from the previous story always complained about his indecisiveness when it came to planning trips or vacations. When she suggested to Yunus that they plan a trip to Florida, he proceeded to enquire about the reasons behind the proposed trip. It took a full hour of discussions before he could be persuaded to undertake the trip. He asserted that he was unwilling to go anywhere unless he could identify a distinct "Why".

In practice…

Islam teaches us to contemplate our actions and the intentions behind them. Before embarking on a trip or engaging in any commitment, Muslims may ask themselves the following questions for self-reflection: "Do I need to proceed on this endeavor?", "Will it benefit my relationship with Allah سبحانه وتعالى ?"," If I die on this trip, what is my intention and how will I answer Allah سبحانه وتعالى ?", etc. According to the prophetic teachings, a person will meet with Allah سبحانه وتعالى in the way and the place where he(she) dies.

25. Sweet and Salty

Hussain used to eat sweet snacks during the daytime and salty snacks at night. When he was asked the reason behind his eating habits. He responded, "The daytime is already bitter. I need to neutralize it with some sweetness. The nighttime is already sweet, and I need to neutralize it with some bitterness."

In practice...

There is always longing for the Divine. Due to daily distractions, a person may not always find avenues to concentrate on the worship and remembrance of Allah سبحانه وتعالى during the daytime. Hence, it can be bitter for those who are disconnected from Allah سبحانه وتعالى. On the contrary, the nights offer dis-engagements from worldly duties, so there is ample time to engage in prayer and remembrance of Allah سبحانه وتعالى. Therefore, it is sweet if one uses the nighttime to connect with the Creator.

26.   Alone in a Crowd

One day, Malik was supplicating to his Sustainer in the front row of the mosque. He was fully immersed in his prayers and basking in the presence of his Creator, until a group of his friends came inside the mosque. When they saw Malik in his signature spot, they began to move towards his direction. Quickly, Malik placed the hood of his jacket over his head. Immediately, they understood the gesture and proceeded to the opposite side of the mosque. He needed his time alone.

In practice...

Privacy within the public space is crucial in maintaining constant companionship with Allah سبحانه وتعالى. If we do not uphold this notion, we will suffer due to detachment from Allah سبحانه وتعالى. This approach is easy to describe but difficult to practice.

27. Humble Gains

One day Mokhtar was not feeling well. He felt distant from the Divine due to the hardness of the heart. Then, he started to reflect on his sins and shortcomings until his tears flowed. As he lay sobbing, he started feeling better and said to himself, *"Astagfirullah."*

In practice…

It is understood in the Islamic tradition that to worship Allah سبحانه وتعالى is a gift from Him and this opportunity should not be taken lightly. Unfortunately, it is quite common for believers to become somewhat arrogant due to their religious growth. The traveler on a journey of spiritual redemption should be in a constant state of vigilance and humility with *'Astagfirullah'*.

28. Sunglasses

Asim was known for his immense wealth. He was often seen wearing expensive clothes. One day, while at the gas station with his kids, he picked up a pair of sunglasses at the cash register and bought them for two dollars. Then, he went to the mosque with his new sunglasses. Everyone in the mosque began to compliment him on his new "designer" sunglasses. Asim chuckled to himself and sought refuge with Allah سبحانه وتعالى from the abode of delusion.

In practice...

Sometimes, on the spiritual path, a person can assume and attribute great value to something that is worthless to God. The external can be deceptive when one assesses its real value. The people's attachment to the world, wealth, and luxury mean nothing in the face of an ephemeral life.

29. The Right Environment

While standing on the street corner, Talha quietly recited his litanies while using prayer beads to keep count. He felt Divine coolness and tranquility each time he asked Allah سبحانه وتعالى to shower blessings and peace on his beloved Prophet Muhammad ﷺ. Meanwhile, the people at the bus stop next to him were engaged in a heated argument. As the altercation escalated, the sounds of curse words and foul language filled the air. Talha placed his beads back in his pocket. He decided he would continue his worship later.

In practice…

In Islamic spirituality, one must guard the senses in order to properly purify the heart. Hence, sometimes, it is better to await an appropriate environment before engaging in serious remembrance of Allah سبحانه وتعالى.

30.   Don't Fill the Vessel

Zainab and Ruquyya decided to share a meal after an Islamic lecture. Zainab ate the food on her plate and refused her friend's offer for a second serving.

Ruquyya: Why are you eating so little?

Zainab: We don't want to undo all that we gained this evening, do we?

In practice…

According to the Islamic traditions, food consumption is not a separate engagement from spirituality. A constantly full stomach strengthens the baser desires and can serve as an obstacle to spiritual growth.

31. Introspection

On a fateful day, Abdullah was late to class. The teacher was upset but did not show his displeasure. Hence, Abdullah immediately engaged in the class discussions, pretending he had been there since the beginning of the class. Halfway through the lecture, his teacher decided to take out the syllabus and review the section on Attendance and Punctuality. Abdullah felt the pain of remorse hit him square in the heart. It was bittersweet.

In practice...

Sometimes, the human nature does not make us receptive in accepting our mistakes and shortcomings. A person on the path is expected to confront all his (her) mistakes in order to repent from them and rectify himself (herself). One of the worst levels of the spiritual path is disregarding one's mistakes or not being aware of them.

32.   Let It Go

After a fallout three years ago, two brothers refused to communicate with one other. Their parents and other siblings had tried to reconcile the two of them, but neither was interested in any amiable resolution of their grievances. Whenever reconciliation was initiated and almost successful, each would begin to recall all the wrong he had endured from the actions of the other, and all prior successes in resolving their grievances will be to no avail.

In practice…

The grief that comes with being unjustly wronged by someone else is quite painful. It is normal to be sad and even shed tears. However, it is unhealthy to hold a grudge for long periods of time. In the long run, this will end up harming you more than the one you have a grudge against.

33.   Highs and Lows

During the holidays, Hamza and Arman once attended their local mosque for Friday prayers. Hamza was captivated by the Imam's speech and he felt an upliftment of his soul during the homily. Midway through the sermon, Arman began to sob loudly. He was thinking about his own shortcomings and ungratefulness to his Lord. It was a very spiritual experience for both.

In practice…

Islamic spirituality is not characterized by mere feelings of elation and happiness. The grief of separation from the Divine and the desire to return to our heavenly abode is also part of our spiritual journey.

34. Backbiting

Naseem was sitting in the mosque. He could clearly hear two people in the back row having a long discussion about a mutual friend. Naseem cringed as the two community members began to dissect their absent companion's flaws. Few minutes into the conversation, one of the two men decided to leave the mosque. Once he was completely gone, the remaining brother walked up to Naseem to give him greetings. He then began to discuss some of the things he did not like about his friend that just exited the mosque. Naseem smiled to himself and asked Allah سبحانه وتعالى for guidance.

In practice...

It is said that the one who backbites about someone else in your presence also backbites about you in your absence. Often, when we speak ill about people, it has little to do with them and more to do about ourselves and our own faults.

35.   Silence

Idris was having a bad week. He decided to vent his frustrations on his brother, Saboor. Every inconvenience, difficulty and mishap that happened to him during the week was a topic of discussion at the dinner table that evening. After a straight hour of complaints, Idris stopped talking and glared angrily at his brother who had not uttered a single word.

"Well do you have anything to say", asked Idris.

"Nope. Not worth the risk", replied Saboor.

In practice…

Muslims believe that they will account for every word that they say in this life. One should only speak with a very specific purpose and with enough consciousness to prevent hurting others. For believers, the default mode for the tongue is silence. If you cannot speak well of someone or something, then do not speak at all.

36.   The Devil in Me

Aws was plagued with a negative thought. He sought refuge in Allah سبحانه وتعالى from the accursed Satan. The incessant thoughts continued. Subsequently, he sought refuge in Allah سبحانه وتعالى from his own self.

In practice…

It is believed that the negative spiritual states of a person are caused either by Satan or the person himself (herself). The symptoms of thoughts from Satan is that they are fleeting and leave when one seeks refuge in Allah سبحانه وتعالى from Satan. Thoughts from the self are incessant and continue unless one embarks on the journey of self-purification.

37. The Night Meetings

Maryam was fastidious about honoring her appointments. The night meetings were essential to her spiritual benefits and growth. It was amazing for someone as insignificant as herself to have a private time when all her issues and problems could be directly addressed. So, she hopped out of bed during the night, went to the bathroom to freshen up. Afterwards, she sat in the middle of her bedroom and began to supplicate to Allah سبحانه وتعالى for all her needs.

In practice…

The nights are important avenues to establish very private and secret relationships with Allah سبحانه وتعالى. Allah سبحانه وتعالى knows all the detailed feelings, fears, emotions and experiences of a person, even if the individual cannot differentiate and name them all. According to one of the Prophetic traditions, Allah سبحانه وتعالى especially establishes a very intimate and powerful relationship with a person in the last one third of the night. The person can get benefit of this relationship if he (she) is awake and speaking to his (her) Lord.

38.   Required Divorce

One local imam was giving a lecture on divorce. He explained the few different cases where it may be necessary or permissible but concluded that divorce should be a last resort. He ended with the following words: "The only required divorce is between you and your whims."

In practice...

Your ego, whims and caprices are more worthy of blame than your spouse, children or anyone else. When a person commences a spiritual journey, the person aims to divorce the ego or self and its constant desire to satisfy its appetites. At the onset of this divorce, the ego can get irritated and can try to hurt you by bombarding you with impulses.

39.   Training the Horse

Adnan spent a great deal of time at his grandfather's rural farm. There were chickens, cows, goats and other livestock. Of all these animals, Adnan's favorite were the horses. During the Summer periods, he would spend the entire day grooming, feeding and riding his grandfather's horses. After a whole day with the beautiful creatures, Adnan would lock the horses in the stables and proceed to the farmhouse for dinner.

One summer evening, after much fun with the horses, he was left with a huge appetite. As he sat at the table with Grandma and Grandpa, he feasted his eyes on a huge plate of chicken wings. His Favorite! Without hesitation, he grabbed a handful of chicken wings and transferred them to his plate. He did this without waiting for his elders to initiate the feasting, which was an established general etiquette in his family. His grandfather simply laughed out loud and remarked, "How did you spend the whole day with the horses and you still cannot control yourself?"

In practice…

In the Islamic tradition, a parable is often drawn between the human ego and a horse. Training the self on the path of spiritual growth is very similar to training a horse. Horses are known to be very stubborn. Yet, they can also be loyal once the proper training procedures are adopted.

40.   Cat and Mouse

Apart from her family members, Fatimah's favorite living being was her cat, Dhakirah. The cat spent most of its day in the backyard, trying to catch the critters that lived in and around the forest behind the house. One afternoon, Fatimah was awaiting a phone call and became very agitated at how long it was taking. She looked out her window and saw Dhakirah crouched in the bushes waiting patiently. It had been in the same position for over an hour. In an instant, a small unsuspecting mouse darted past and Dhakirah immediately snatched up the prey. Fatimah watched in awe and contemplated the inner meaning behind the incident. The reality hit her. She wept profusely and sought patience from Allah سبحانه وتعالى.

In practice…

It is very important to constantly observe nature as there are numerous lessons and signs in all of creations. Active reflection is designed to increase one's knowledge on the spiritual path.

41.   Strength and Weakness

On the floor of his room, Jabbir got back on his knees and prepared himself for another round of pushups. Over the past few months, he had developed the routine of completing 1000 pushups each day. He broke these pushups into sets of 50 and spread them throughout the entire day. He was currently on his last set. After completing the last 50 pushups with ease, he hopped up smiling. He asked Allah سبحانه وتعالى to forgive him and he thanked his Creator for the strength granted to him.

In practice…

It is very important to acknowledge that all our physical and spiritual prowess are gifts from Allah سبحانه وتعالى. In other words, the person should believe that nothing can be attained or achieved without the blessings and openings from Allah سبحانه وتعالى. There are several prayers that people recite to instill this notion into the heart. In the story, Jabbir sought forgiveness from his Lord to remind him of the reality of his situation.

42.   Prepare for the Storm

Things were going well in Jamal's life. An outsider would immediately recognize his material and spiritual success. Things eventually got so smooth in his life, that he began to get concerned. At 3:30 am one night, his phone alarm went off. He leapt out of bed with his "game-face" on. He went to the bathroom and thoroughly performed his ablution. Right before starting his night prayers, he checked off the notification on the screen of his phone. It indicated: "Training".

In practice…

Humans have great difficulty in interpreting the evils, pains, and difficulties experienced in life. A purpose of the spiritual path is to train the self and ego before encountering these tests. If we fail to adorn proper clothing in a freezing weather, we may lose our organs or limbs. Similarly, if a person is accustomed to an indulgence in his (her) desires, it will be difficult to deal with inconvenience or hardship. If we fail to acquire the spiritual training of heart and mind through practicing different rituals, we stand the risk of losing faith due to our inability to handle the numerous tests we are bound to encounter.

43. Bad Words

Ahmed and Zakariyya came into the mosque for their Quran class, arguing with each other about who was the better wrestler. Their debate grew to be quite intense and various insults were exchanged between them. Once Imam Suleiman walked in, the conversation ended, and the boys began to memorize their allotted page for the day.

Ahmed began to tell his teacher about the difficult he was having with his memorization. His teacher said, "You made a choice. Good and bad words cannot co-exist at the same time in the heart." The teacher further explained, "If you indulge in a single bad word, all good words and your memorization will elude you."

In practice...

The human heart is a vessel that has the capacity to hold whatever is placed in it. However, there are certain contents that do not co-exist. The Quran is pure and clean. A person will have difficulty if his (her) tongue and mind engages in anger, backbiting, jealousy and any other despicable act. This notion is much embedded in the advice of Prophet Muhammad (ﷺ) for the ones who desire to memorize the Quran.

44.   The Stench of Arrogance

There was a very poor person who regularly came to the mosque with a foul odor. The congregants did not want to embarrass him. One day, this individual came to the mosque and stood right next to Naji. During his prayer, Naji began thinking, "Lucky Me. Of all the people he decided to stand next to…". As soon as he began having these thoughts, Naji's concentration in his prayer began to diminish and this continued throughout the prayer. After the prayer, Naji asked Allah سبحانه وتعالى for forgiveness and sought refuge from discouraging the presence of angels with the stench of his arrogance.

In practice…

Sometimes, if a person thinks badly about others, or has feelings of arrogance, the bad thoughts have a metaphysical foulness that drives off angels. These angels provide inspiration to the heart of righteous believers and their desertion can lead to a spiritual downfall. Hence, one should guard the heart from thinking ill of others.

45. Stay in Good Spirits

After the Friday sermon, the congregants of the mosque began to move out from the prayer space into the masjid lobby in droves. No sooner than five minutes after the service ended, an argument ensued between two gentlemen who collided with each other at the shoe rack. Voices were raised and mild expletives were exchanged. Yusuf witnessed this unfortunate scene and he sought refuge in Allah سبحانه وتعالى from the accursed Satan and asked Him for support against unseen armies. Thereafter, he went to intervene in the altercation.

In practice…

When there is acrimony among people, then that environment is contaminated with bad spirits instead of the angelic beings. Bad spirits encourage bad words, altercations, anger, and physical harm. Angelic beings inspire good words, peaceful feelings and general tranquility. Yusuf asked Allah سبحانه وتعالى to send His angels to turn the tide in the spiritual battle.

46.   Be Careful - Fragile

Abdul Kareem and his dad, Ibrahim, were clearing out the garage. As they placed items in the large garbage container outside the enclosure, Abdul Kareem came across a large bag of old glass cups. He chucked the entire bag in the garbage can only to be met with the sound of cracking glass. His father yelled at him for his lack of care. Abdul Kareem responded, "What's the issue? They are going to the trash anyway". Ibrahim said calmly, "Some people are more fragile than glass. It's better you start practicing now."

In practice...

Prophet Muhammad (ﷺ) was the gentlest of people. It is said that his tenderness extended to both the living and the nonliving. The prophetic character is holistic and extends to all creations.

47.   Hold onto the Rope

One day, Habeeb was out at sea taking a class with some professional divers. Nearby, there were few amateur divers diving through very deep depths of the sea on their own. These divers were connected to their vessel by tethers. However, Habeeb could see that one of the divers from the group had chosen to dive without being tethered to the vessel.

Close to the end of his class, Habeeb realized that an emergency speedboat had arrived the scene where the amateur divers were once located. A few of them were still there and they were all weeping. When he got close enough to enquire what happened, he was informed that the diver that refused to use a tether while diving almost drowned in the sea. He was unconscious and was now being taken to the hospital.

In practice…

In the story, the victim may have good intentions, but he failed to follow the rules and almost lost his life. Similarly, in the life of a Muslim, the pillars of the faith are like tethers. The goal is that we expand on the pillars without destroying or removing them. One cannot break the rules of the religion or the basic creed under the guise of spiritual development.

48.   The Right Perspective

On his way out of his house, Saeed collided with an object in his

patio. He cursed his bad luck and started walking towards the mosque. As

he limped up the stairs of the mosque, out of the corner of his right eye, he

sighted a figure moving very slowly. He turned around to behold an older

man whose right leg was completely amputated, going up the stairs with the

aid of crutches. Saeed thanked Allah سبحانه وتعالى for his circumstance.

"*Alhamdulillah!*"

In practice…

Showing appreciations without any complaints in the relationship

with Allah سبحانه وتعالى is of utmost importance. The phrase *Alhamdulillah*

(All praises belong to God) emphasizes this notion of showing appreciation

to the Divine under all circumstances. In the story, the old disabled man

was struggling to enter the mosque, which served as a reminder to Saeed on

how fortunate he really was. Sometimes, people look at what is not within

their reach and complain. Rather, they should appreciate the numerous

blessings of the Creator and be thankful to Him.

49.   Adjust Your Frames

One night, Basheer had a dream. In his dream, he was trying to see the road ahead of him, but it was blurry. There was residue on his eyeglass that was distorting the image. Suddenly, his local imam grabbed the eyeglass off his face, wiped it clean and told him to look again. The straight road was now clear. It was leading straight to a garden. Basheer woke from the dream. He immediately sought forgiveness from his Lord for his misconceptions.

In practice…

In the dream, Basheer was unable to see clearly because of the eyeglass he was wearing. The eyeglass is a metaphor for our limited cognitive abilities or viewpoints about things. Sometimes, they prevent us from seeing the straight path. So, we often need a teacher to help remove these doubts and allow us to see clearly again.

50.   The Ant and the Carpet

Zainab decided to spend the afternoon in the mosque. She examined an ant walking on the carpet. The carpet was nice and green with some intricate designs. Zainab pondered on how it must feel like to live in a green world. She then sought guidance from the One who knows the extent of what is beyond her actual world.

In practice…

In the story, the ant was on a two-dimensional plane (carpet). In contrast to the ant, Zainab could see the carpet within the context of the larger room. Zainab was above the carpet, looking down, but decided to view things from an ant's perspectives. Likewise, human understanding cannot completely comprehend Divine knowledge.

51.   Speak Well or Remain Silent

Imam Zaid had just finished leading his congregation in the sunset prayer. As soon as he finished, a rude man stepped out of the prayer line and began to criticize the Imam for the subtle mistakes in his pronunciation during recitation. In reality, the man was uninformed about the existence and validity of different recitation styles that were all directly transmitted from Prophet Muhammad (ﷺ). Imam Zaid opened his mouth to correct the ignorant man. But once he saw how upset the latter was, the imam decided to keep quiet and acknowledge the critique without responding.

In practice…

It is always important to reflect and think well before uttering any word to anyone. Muslims prefer silence and only engage in purposeful conversations when necessary. If they find themselves in any difficult situation, they use wisdom to minimize arguments.

52.   We All Slip

Hud often mocked his brother, Salih, for the latter's clumsiness. Over many years of living together, Hud had lost track of the number of eyeglasses his younger brother had broken and how many times he had slipped down the stairs. Hud would often find himself lecturing Salih on the importance of situational awareness and being attentive. He would also express displeasure in his brother's shortcomings.

One day, Hud was scolding his brother in the kitchen and began pacing back and forth. He was so engrossed with criticizing Salih's faults that he did not notice a water spill on the floor. As he took one step towards the little puddle, he slipped and fell flat on his face. As Hud stood up, his face flushed red in embarrassment. Then, he thanked Allah سبحانه وتعالى for manifesting his own arrogance to him.

In practice…

It is said that the arrogance that results in judging people for a sin is worse than the sin itself. Instead of thanking Allah سبحانه وتعالى for not testing him with awkwardness like his brother, Hud allowed himself to become pompous. His fall is interpreted as a reminder from Allah سبحانه وتعالى of his own weakness.

53. The Grass is Greener on the Other Side

What a letdown! Adeeb and his family had been planning to move from their home country of Pakistan to England for over three years. For those three years, their planned travel was all Adeeb could talk about each day. The teenager spent most of his time immersed in the British culture. Everything from the English soccer clubs to the British street slangs captured his imagination. However, his first two months in his new country was nothing he had ever imagined. The weather was dull and dreary. Unlike the close-knit school he attended in Pakistan, his new school environment was cold and unfriendly. His life had changed drastically. Adeeb had learnt his lesson. He would no longer make judgments from the outside.

In practice…

In the story, Adeeb had a false expectation of life in England. His over-reliance on popular media as a primary source of information was blameworthy. Often in life, things look great on the outside. But once you get closer, there are lots of underlining issues that you must contend with.

54. The Same End

Ismail always spent his weekends volunteering alongside his mom at a nursing home. While there, he would often witness unsightly and disturbing things. Due to their old age, the tenants would often burp, fart and drool unexpectedly. Ismail being a young teen, was somewhat immature and initially found this to be comical. One Saturday afternoon, his mom observed his reaction and decided to end his amusement with a single question: "What do you think will happen when you are older?" Ismail's smile vanished.

In practice...

In the story, Ismail's mother reminded him that he would face the same issues the seniors were currently grappling with when he became older. As humans, we may have instant negative feelings and thoughts towards others. However, these are not harmful if they don't become permanent and are rejected as soon as they manifest.

55.   How to Get Everything

Nuh brought his three daughters into the living room for a surprise. In the room were eight wrapped packages. "Here are the rules," said their smiling father. He continued, "You can pick one item in the room and it is yours. The catch is that you can only pick one item." His two older daughters, Ruquyya and Mariam, immediately ran towards each box and started to shake them to check their content. Nuh's youngest daughter ran up to him, grabbed his hands and laughed, "I pick you, Dad". "If I get you, I get all the gifts". Nuh lowered his head down and began to sob. He then quietly supplicated to Allah سبحانه وتعالى for his bounties.

In practice…

Islam teaches us not to chase after material things. If one pleases Allah سبحانه وتعالى, Allah سبحانه وتعالى can give boundless rewards in this world and the next. Nuh's daughter made a statement that reminded him of this reality, and he interpreted it as a sign from his Maker to turn back to Him.

56.   Change is Good

Ameerah and Hind had just arrived back in their hometown after their first year in college. They decided to meet up over coffee and reminisce on old times. Within half an hour of speaking, Ameerah realized that Hind had changed a lot while away. She was no longer using foul language and phrases like *inshaAllah* and *mashaAllah* were now abound in her speech. Afterwards, Ameerah remarked to her friend how much she had changed. Hind responded with a single word, *"Alhamdulillah"*.

In practice...

In Islam, personal change and growth is always a good thing. Each day, a person is expected to go further in the closeness and union with God. The only unchanged One is Allah سبحانه وتعالى. On the other hand, humans should strive to become better and not be concerned with what others think.

57. Torturing the Text

Sara had just bought a book of poems by her favorite poet, Rumi. Rumi was an Islamic scholar who wrote poems about the love of Allah سبحانه وتعالى with frequent use of metaphor. Each time she had read the poems in the past, she felt a spiritual awakening in her heart. And it had a taste that was sweeter than honey. However, she failed to realize that the copy she just bought was translated by an atheist academic who had taken it upon himself to provide an added commentary. Sara tried reading the book. The sweetness was nowhere found.

In practice...

Teachings of the Islamic tradition are meant to be believed and implemented. Those who are skeptical or have no intention of implementing them, will be barred from the benefit of Islamic poetry or literature. It is important to seek religious counsel and benefit from those who believe and live what they are speaking about.

58.   Smart as a Devil

The scores for the high school's IQ test had just been released. Word spread quickly that Faheem had gotten the highest score in the school's long history. Everyone was complementing and praising him for his high intellect throughout the entire day. When Faheem got home, he told his parents the good news. His parents congratulated him, and his mother went to prepare a special meal to celebrate. Meanwhile, Faheem sat in the living room with his father. Then, his father said something very peculiar. He said: "I am happy for your accomplishment. Just be sure to stay close to the earth. Don't rise like fire."

Faheem pondered what the meaning could be.

In practice…

Islam encourages the use of the intellect more than most religious traditions. However, unrestricted use of the intellect constitutes a type of arrogance. This is the trap that Satan fell into in the Quranic account where he chose not to bow to Adam despite being commanded to do so by Allah سبحانه وتعالى. He used his own false logic by stating that he was better than Adam because he was created from fire and the latter was created from clay. The intellect can be a curse when it is used to circumvent Divine injunctions. Faheem's father was alluding to this fact.

61

59.   Merciful Outlook

It had only been one hour. Myles had decided to leave the handyman working in his house for one hour. Now, he had come back, and the handyman had absconded with few pieces of expensive furniture. Myles had no idea what could have caused the worker to do such a deplorable thing. However, after giving it some thought, he thought that if the man was desperate enough to rob him, he must have needed the money. As he went to file the police report, he asked Allah سبحانه وتعالى to forgive the man.

In practice…

Having a good opinion of people is a signature trait of the righteous. Many pious people of the past, upon being asked why they did not retaliate orally against those who wronged them, responded by saying that "a vessel can only bring forth that which is within it". In other words, a pure heart will only produce pure words.

60.   At Each Level

Guled spent the entire summer shadowing Imam Jibreel. His favorite part about the experience was watching how caring the community leader was to his local community. However, there was one particularly strange thing that he noticed. Often, Imam Jibreel would provide different answers to different people for the same question on different occasions. When Guled asked his imam why he was doing this, Imam Jibreel smiled and asked a rhetorical question: "Does the same key work for every lock?"

In practice…

Prophet Muhammad (ﷺ) was sent with a message for all mankind. He used to speak to all classes of his society and regularly modified his language and delivery to suit his audience. Speaking the truth is not the only criteria when admonishing others. If others cannot understand or relate to your advice, then you may be doing them a disservice by attempting to advise them.

61.   False Gratitude

Ridwan was really enjoying the time spent at the monthly family dinner. All his siblings, uncles, aunts and their children were in his parents' house for a huge meal. The only issue was listening to his uncle's ceaseless complaints about the food: "There isn't enough salt," "There is too much spice." And the list went on. Once his uncle finished his meal, he called Ridwan to collect his plate. Ridwan giggled. Not because he was asked to collect the plate, but because his uncle said "*Alhamdulillah*" after finishing the meal.

In practice…

Expressions have their meanings. If we don't act according to the meanings of the Islamic statements we proclaim, then we do not get the full benefits. '*Alhamdullillah*' (All praises belong to God) is an expression that reminds us to avoid complaining, but to show appreciations. When the statement is expressed, it affects the heart and mind, and thereby influences our behavior.

62. Deaf to Sin

Arman sat in the living room with his grandfather. His grandfather was very old, and his sense organs were beginning to fail him. Grandpa's sight was fading, and he could barely hear at all. Arman often felt bad when he saw his grandfather's condition and thanked his Creator for his own situation. However, today was a little different. When a neighbor came over for dinner, he had a lot to say. And none of it was palatable. As the neighbor backbit and slandered half of the people in the entire neighborhood, Arman sat in an awkward silence. For the first time, Arman wished he could switch places with his grandfather.

In practice...

The main purposes of hearing are listening to beneficial things and seeking the signs of your Lord. When we listen to inappropriate conversations, we have misused one of our Lord's blessings and exposed our souls to harm. Arman realized this when he was subjected to the ill speech of his neighbor.

63.   It is Not Personal

There was an elder in the mosque who loved to teach the kids. Often, he would be stern to get them to behave well. Although the teacher appeared angry to an outsider, the kids seemed to love him. The amount of care he showed over the years allowed them to realize his true intents. The kids did not interpret their beloved teacher's treatment as abuse or hate, but as his way of showing his care and concern. And they loved him even more for it.

In practice...

Refinement of the human character is a major objective of the prophetic mission. This can involve nurturing the children and instilling discipline in them. It is important for children to realize that this is not meant to hurt them. Rather, it is meant to help them in the long run.

64.   Foundation First

Tariq considered much of his Islamic studies class to be very boring. Learning the details on how to properly make *wudhu* and the difference between major and minor impurity seemed irrelevant. The only part he really liked was when Imam Yasir spoke about the lofty character of Prophet Muhammad (ﷺ) and the incidents in his life. Hearing about the virtues of the best of creation (ﷺ) and how he overcame difficulties, motivated Tariq and gave him inspirations. When he communicated his thoughts to Imam Yasir, the imam responded by saying: "If you can't emulate the Prophet Muhammad (ﷺ) in his *wudhu*, do you think you can emulate him (ﷺ) in patience?

In practice…

Islam is built on five pillars. Although the religion encompasses much more than these, we cannot abandon them and expect to grow spiritually. We must start with foundational practices even if they are somewhat mundane or undesirable. Through this, we will attain higher ranks.

65.   Language of the Heart

Willie was sitting on the front porch of his house, looking at the birds in the sky and listening to his favorite Quran reciter when his neighbor, Joshua, walked by. The following conversation ensued:

Joshua: You are always listening to that. Do you even know what it means?

Willie: Some of it, but not all of it.

Joshua: Then, how do you expect to benefit from it?

Willie: Do you know precisely every ingredient in an Aspirin tablet and its function?

When Joshua could not respond in the affirmative, Willie asked: Does it still work for you?

Joshua: Yes.

Willie: Well, consider this to be medicine for the soul.

In practice…

It is encouraged to listen to and recite the Quran in its original language of revelation. Although the listener may not be a native speaker of the Arabic language, the Divine speech has great effects on the heart and mind of the listener even if he (she) doesn't fully understand their meanings. When we make conscious efforts to learn the meanings of the phrases, then the effects of spiritual engagement can increase.

66.   Book of Life

Bilal reflected on the last few years of his life: its highs and lows, its eases and difficulties, the expected and the unexpected. It was like a novel. He just prayed to the Author for a good ending.

In practice...

Allah سبحانه وتعالى alternates the conditions of his servants in order to bring them back to Him and Him alone. The roller coaster experience of our earthly sojourn is inconsequential when compared to either eternal bliss or perpetual punishment in the next life.

67.   Walking Quran

Abdul Hafiz was known to recite the Quran everywhere he visited. He would recite at home, work, school and the park. He would recite standing, sitting, and reclining. If he was awake and not in conversation with anyone, he was reciting the Quran. And more impressively, he always recited from memory. Abdul Hafiz was...well...a Hafiz! In other words, he had committed the entirety of the Quran to memory. One Ramadan, Abdul Hafiz spent his last ten days in the masjid for *itikahf.* As he slept in the afternoon, some of the people present observed him while in slumber. To their bewilderment, his lips were still moving in the recitation of the Quran.

In practice...

Our goal is to recite, teach and learn until the sacred knowledge becomes second nature to us- until it becomes part of our mind, heart and soul. This is the wisdom behind the heavy emphasis on memorization in the Islamic tradition.

68.   Sigh of Regret

Abdul Tawwab was running late for the congregational prayer. Praying the *Isha salah* in his local mosque was the highlight of his day. It was his chosen time for unwinding and releasing all his stress and concerns. Once he entered the mosque, he realized the *salah* had already been concluded. He was distraught. He let out a huge sigh of remorse. An old man in the front row of the mosque walked right up to him and said: "I would happily trade the rewards of the prayer I just preformed for the sigh of grief that you just let out."

In practice…

The primary goal in our earthly sojourn is to submit to our Creator and to do what he loves. Allah سبحانه وتعالى loves his servants to be remorseful and humble. He does not want us to be haughty or proud. Sometimes, a sin that humbles you is far better than a good deed that makes you arrogant.

69.   Not Your Property

Abdul Razzaq had just left this world. He was a pious man whose generosity was legendary in his community. A total of seven children survived him. The inheritance he left behind included a huge house, several vehicles and a large sum of money. There was enough to be easily shared amongst his wife and children. His Lord had certainly given him a great bounty. And what a great loan it was.

In practice...

Your life and everything in it are trusts from your Creator. The mere fact that you will be separated from all your blessings is a clear indication that it was never yours in the first place. Anything you have is a blessing provided to aid your success in the test of life. It is important to see reality for what it is before you are forced to acknowledge the truth.

70.   It is Like Magic

Harun had a bad stomachache. So, he did what a typical nine-year old would do - He complained to his mother. She picked him up, recited some verses of the Quran, and blew on his stomach. Shortly after, Harun felt better. He thanked his mother and exclaimed, "It is just like magic!". His mother laughed and responded: "Actually, it is the exact opposite."

In practice...

If the Quran is recited with firm faith, it could have a curative effect on one's ailments. It is also a means to protect us from magic and evil machinations. Muslims believe in the existence of magic, but it is a forbidden art and Allah سبحانه وتعالى cursed those who are involved in it.

71.   Just a Drop

After the Friday night masjid gathering, Yaseen and his father,

Suhaib, went out for ice cream. While slurping their sundaes, they spoke

about their past week and their expectations for the week ahead. The

environment was very light, and they indulged in jokes and witticism.

Caught up in the moment, Yaseen started to speak ill of a classmate.

Immediately, Suhaib scolded his son for backbiting. "I know it is wrong,

but backbiting just this one time won't hurt", responded Yaseen. "How

about just pouring a single drop of urine in your sundae?," asked Suhaib.

Yaseen fell silent. He got the hint.

In practice...

A person cannot purposefully commit an evil deed and expect a

good outcome. Even though the outcome may look alluring, such deeds

have undesirable effects on the states of our hearts. In the story, Suhaib

reminded his son how a single slip can ruin an entire spiritual state.

72.   Pass the Test

Sawda couldn't help but notice that it was quite a rough year for her friend, Hajera. Her grandmother died earlier during the year. She had already gotten seriously ill three times. Now, after a discussion with her school counselor, she discovered that due to her last test score, she was going to fail the senior Math class. What amazed Sawda the most was that she had never heard Hajera complain about anything. When she asked Hajera the reason behind her fortitude, her friend replied: "Yes, I failed my math test. Let me, at least, pass my real test."

In practice…

One of the most praiseworthy character traits is patience. When difficulty befalls a person, if he (she) does not complain but recognizes that his (her) situation is from Allah سبحانه وتعالى, then such a person can use the unfortunate incidence as an opportunity to excel spiritually. Although in practice, we all ask for a good and an easy life, we should always subscribe to patience if we experience calamities. In both good and bad situations, we should appreciate the relationship with Allah سبحانه وتعالى.

73. Check your Heart

Khalid loved to listen to Islamic lectures as he and his daughter, Amina, drove home. He kept a playlist with a selection of scholars speaking on different topics. They have a long commute, so they would listen to the lectures during the first half of the drive and then engage in discussions related to the lectures during the other half. This afternoon, Amina was not impressed with the speaker. She told her father that she felt his message was not relevant to the present times. Khalid replied: "Perhaps, we should first check our own hearts".

In practice…

Throughout history, people have been heedless of the warnings and teachings brought to them by the prophets. There were no faults in the messengers or the Divine texts. Rather, the people were not receptive to the messengers and the Divine texts they brought. Sometimes, those who convey a message may have some personal shortcomings, but we should focus on the message or the admonition.

74.   Clear the Weeds

Abu Bakr was leaving for his *Umrah* trip in two weeks. His friends kept telling him how important it was for him to quickly sort out the trip logistics. However, each time they saw Abu Bakr, he was either sitting in a corner with his beads asking Allah سبحانه وتعالى for forgiveness or on the phone calling people he had previously offended. Everyone he had ever had a quarrel with was guaranteed to receive a call from him. During the call, he would apologize and seek their pardon. When his friends asked why he was not spending his time to prepare for his trip, his answer was always the same: "I am, but I cannot expect to plant flowers before I clear the weeds."

In practice...

As humans, we are not immune to sins and vices. These wrongdoings taint our hearts and deeds. They prevent good deeds (such as performing *Umrah*) from having their full desired effects. Hence, it is recommended to repent and rectify our wrongdoings before engaging in any important good deed.

75.   Third World Countries

Aisha was a regular volunteer at the refugee center. She loved to help people. She appreciated the resilience and beautiful characters of the people she was helping. One day, while on her way home from the shelter house, a friend approached her and said, "I feel bad for these refugees. I wonder what it must be like to come from an underdeveloped country." Aisha smiled and said, "I feel worse for those with underdeveloped souls."

In practice...

In Islam, we place more emphasis on spiritual growth and not material growth. The one with good character and a connection to the Creator has everything. The one with immense wealth and comfort, but a foul temperament and weak faith has nothing.

76.   Interfaith

Shaykh Zubair was patiently waiting for his opportunity to address the interfaith meeting. The organizers had drawn lots among the speakers to decide the order to respond to a question and Shaykh Zubair came up last. The question was simple: "What is the purpose of life according to your religious tradition?" At this point during the meeting, the priest had already spoken, and the rabbi was midway in his response. Each of the cleric was going into subtleties of his religious tradition and providing answers that were quite nebulous. The meeting attendees were in rapt attention, but most of them seemed confused. Once it was Shaykh Zubair's turn to speak, he smiled and provided only a three-word response: "To know God!".

In practice…

The Quran clearly states that Allah سبحانه وتعالى created humans to worship Him. Early Quranic exegesis by one of the famous companions of Prophet Muhammad (ﷺ) says that to worship Allah سبحانه وتعالى means to know Him. Islam is unique in that the general creed and worldview is extremely simple and accessible to the general public.

77. Miss Your Meeting

It was indeed a sad day at Abbas's house. His family had just received the tragic news that his cousin had died in a car crash. His cousin was driving fast to avoid missing a scheduled meeting at work and was hit by a truck while on the highway. He was only 25 at the time. Abbas was grief stricken and was struggling to process the recent event. After the funeral prayers, Abbas asked his father: "Why did he have to go so young?". Abbas's father said curtly: "He couldn't miss his meeting."

In practice...

Regardless of what we occupy ourselves with in this world, we are all moving towards our demise. Our transition from the world involves a long journey that starts in the grave, leads to the Day of Resurrection, and finally ends in a meeting with Allah سبحانه وتعالى. It is a meeting that cannot be avoided. Although we cannot predict its scheduled time, it is our duty to spend our lives preparing for this meeting.

78. The Teacher

Haytham was about three hours away from his home. He was driving back home after visiting his teacher. It was a 5-hour drive from his home to his teacher's residence. It was his normal practice to undertake this trip once a month on a weekend, and he would sit with the elder for a full afternoon. They would eat lunch and Haytham would ask for advice. Sometimes, the visit would last for only an hour. Then, Haytham would make the long drive back home, but he never regretted it for a single moment.

In practice...

In the Islamic tradition, scholars and teachers play a pivotal role in the knowledge seeking process. They are living examples of the desirable traits we read in the Islamic literature. There are certain benefits derived from keeping the company of these people that can never be replicated from just reading the Islamic books. When we identify those that can benefit us spiritually, it is worth the struggle to seek their company and interact with them. It is not uncommon to gain more benefit in a few days spent in the company of the learned than from several months (or even years) spent in a self-directed learning immersion.

79. Blessed Food

Mahfoud was in a conversation with his mother in the kitchen while they were preparing the family dinner. Mahfoud was worried because winter was quickly approaching. He always got very ill as soon as the temperature dropped. Upon hearing him express this concern, his mother smiled and said: "You know what the solution is, right?". "What?" asked Mahfoud. "Preventative medicine," replied his mother while chuckling. She then began to recite a verse of the Quran over the food as she cooked.

In practice...

The recitation of the Quran and the remembrance of Allah سبحانه وتعالى have a metaphysical effect on the things and people around it. Reciting the Quran (or *salawat* on the Prophet Muhammad (ﷺ) over food) is a good way to increase blessings in our lives and improve our health.

80.   Avoiding Claims

This evening's *Hadith* class in the mosque was on the narration where Prophet Muhammad (ﷺ) stated that, "The scholars are the inheritors of the prophets." Shaykh Hakeem had studied all over the Muslim world and was able to quote extensively from several *Hadiths-* all from memory. He was also a man of impeccable character and devotion. As he explained that the scholars are the bearers of prophetic knowledge, the students sat in awe. One young man asked: "O Shaykh, does that mean that you are a representative of Prophet Muhammad (ﷺ)?" The Shaykh frowned and said: "I am not a scholar. I am only a student of knowledge just like yourselves." The students smiled. This is exactly why they all loved their beloved Shaykh.

In practice…

Although genuine Islamic teachers are spiritually blessed and the students revere them a lot, they see themselves at a low spiritual level in order to avoid any entrapment due to arrogance. Genuine humility of the teacher is one of the character traits of a good teacher.

81.   Chain of Command

Salem was having a discussion on religious knowledge and its sources with some of his friends from other faith traditions. The conversation was filled with phrases like: "I think", "My opinion is", "My feelings on the topic are", etc. This gathering was very different from what Salem was accustomed to. In Salem's circle, you are more likely to hear: "Allah سبحانه وتعالى says" and "his Prophet Muhammad (ﷺ) says."

In practice…

Islam does not prohibit having personal opinions. However, the foundation of Islamic knowledge lies in the Quran and Prophetic teachings (i.e. *Sunnah*), followed by the interpretations of the early generations. If you do not reference the Quran and *Sunnah* in the Islamic scholastic realm, then your presentations are worth but little.

82. Uncertainty in your Certainty

Salman had a Christian friend. They once had a discussion on the attainment of salvation in this world and the afterlife. His friend said, "If a person has the correct belief, then he (she) can be saved." Salman added, "I agree. However, this is not a certainty until the person dies. Creed is your foundation. Then, you build upon it with deeds."

In practice...

If the person has the right belief and complements it with good action, then he (she) can be rewarded and saved from punishment. However, this possibility is not certain. The idea is that a person does not really know the reality of his (her) intention or sincerity in performing good actions. There are lots of stories in the Islamic tradition of people who were apparently prodigious worshippers of Allah سبحانه وتعالى but were thrown to the hellfire as a result of show off, condescension, arrogance, etc. Conversely, there are stories about the people who were in obvious (external) disobedience to Allah سبحانه وتعالى but were forgiven by Allah سبحانه وتعالى due to their (internal) sincere intention. Although, there is a general rule in the scriptures that those with the right belief and action can be saved, Islam teaches us to be wary of our real intentions. Moreover, there is no certainty that we will die in the state of Islam. This notion of

uncertainty always keeps one alert and humble.

83.   Protect Your Valuables

Fuad and Aqil were going for a walk in the park. Fuad was strolling leisurely, completely relaxed and oblivious of his surroundings. On the other hand, Aqil was very tense, cautious, and alert. He intended to make a large purchase after their walk, so he was walking around with a few hundred dollars in his pocket. The tension weighed on Aqil, but he had no complaints. If you have something valuable, you must be willing to guard it. He asked Allah سبحانه وتعالى for increase in faith and for the ability to safeguard it.

In practice...

The story revolves around the metaphor of your faith being your most valuable possession. As your faith grows, you become more particular about guarding it. You become more particular about the places you go and the types of people you interact with.

84.   The Perfect Fit

Adeeb entered his grandfather's house for the Eid gathering. In the first hour, he:

i.   Kissed his grandparents' hands.

ii.   Gave his uncles and aunts hugs.

iii.   Patted his younger cousins on the head.

iv.   Held his baby cousin in his arms.

v.   Scratched the cat behind the ears.

"Just like a key in lock," thought Adeeb to himself about his actions. All different but all perfectly suited for the situation.

In practice…

It is essential to imbibe the right etiquettes of daily interactions in relation to different people and within different contexts. This is called *adab*. It is especially important to learn the etiquettes related to our relationships with our teachers, lectures and peers. Having the right *adab* ultimately helps us establish a relationship with God.

85.   The Cost of Time

Hamid did all his shopping online. Often, his friends would alert him to the existence of better bargain deals in nearby stores. Hamid explained to them that his online purchases came straight to the house. Then, he said: "Whatever money you save from your visit to the store is being lost to the time you spent to get there." Thereafter, he smirked, "That doesn't sound like a deal to me!"

In practice…

In this life, your time is your capital. It is the most valuable thing you have. You cannot get it back after you have lost it, and no one can forcefully take it from you. However, because we are constantly experiencing it, we fail to appreciate it.

86. Permanent Love

Abdul Wudud sat in his family's new living room, sobbing quietly. They had just moved to the suburbs few weeks ago. Abdul Wudud now had a new house, a new school and new friends. He pretty much had a new life. And to be honest, it was not all that bad. His new house is bigger than the old one. His new school is one of the best private schools in the country. He now also has new friends, but they were not his old friends.

In practice...

Close companionship among the people is a hallmark feature of the prophetic teachings and lifestyle. However, Muslims should always ensure they keep their main connection with the Lord of the Worlds, even in the absence of their fellow believers. Prophet Muhammad (ﷺ) says, "Love whomever you wish, for you will be separated. Know that the nobility of the believer is in prayer at night, and his honor is in his independence of the people."

87.   Admired by the Prophets

Mustafa loved his youth group's events. From weekly classes to annual knowledge retreats, every program organized by the masjid was full of benefit. Mustafa loved sacred knowledge and could not get enough of it. For this month's trip, Mustafa, Imam Yahya and some of the other brothers visited a nearby community. When they got there, there was a huge dinner awaiting them. It was a very relaxed atmosphere with good food and good company. However, Mustafa was not at ease. He felt that if he was not directly learning prophetic knowledge, then he must be wasting his time. He expressed his concern to Imam Yahya. Imam Yahya smiled and said: "Mustafa, right now, we are admired by the prophets and the martyrs." Mustafa stared back at the Imam in confusion. Imam Yahya began to narrate a *Hadith*…

In practice…

Prophet Muhammad (ﷺ) said Allah سبحانه وتعالى said: "Those who love each other for the sake of my glory will be upon pulpits of light, admired by the prophets and the martyrs." The path to the pleasure of Allah سبحانه وتعالى is in following the prophetic teachings. That includes visiting your brothers (sisters) and loving them for His sake.

91

88.   Piercing Insight

Lut was trying to keep a straight face. His mom had specifically instructed him not to touch the sumptuous plate of chocolates on the table. She said the delicacies were for the guests and that it was bad etiquette to eat before their guests. But he was so hungry. And he just couldn't resist the chocolates. So, he ate a few and rearranged the chocolates on the plate to conceal his action. Now, the only thing left was to make sure he didn't look suspicious.

When his mom walked into the room, he was sitting at the dining table, working on his homework. His mom moved towards the next room. She almost opened the door to the next room before she suddenly stopped in her tracks. Then, she glared at Lut. He tried to stay focused on his homework. "What did you do?", his mom yelled. Lut let out a sigh of exasperation. He was unsure how she knew, but somehow, she always seems to know when he is up to mischief.

In practice…

If it is not enough to know that Allah سبحانه وتعالى is watching us, then we should realize that many righteous believers are known to have deep insights of the human nature. The Prophet Muhammad (ﷺ) said,

"Beware of the intuition of the believer. Verily, he sees with the light of

Allah سبحانه وتعالى."

89.   Learn to Flow

Before they could go Whitewater rafting, Arkan and his friends were mandated to take a short course on safety precautions and procedures. One section of the course explained what to do when rafters fall out of the raft. The instructor explained that if anyone is caught in a fast-moving water, the worst thing to do is to try and swim against the water currents. As unintuitive as it might seem, the best thing you can do in that situation is to flow with the currents. Upon hearing this, Arkan was taken aback. He reflected on the difficult of accepting the inevitable.

In practice…

One of the six articles of faith is to believe in the Divine Decree- in all its good and bad. In other words, everything (past, present and future) has been ordained for you before your creation. Thus, in Islam, although we take the means, we are also taught to accept what Allah سبحانه وتعالى is facilitating for us.

90.   Knocking on the Door

She rang the bell, but no one answered the door. They were supposed to be home. Once again, she rang the bell. Maybe the bell was broken. So, she knocked the door. Once. Twice. Thrice. Still no answer. She smiled to herself and sought refuge in Allah سبحانه وتعالى from a supplication that is not accepted.

In practice…

We do our part by asking Allah سبحانه وتعالى to aid us in our affairs. However, it is important to remember that the answer belongs to Him and Him alone. The character in the story considered knocking on the door as a metaphor for asking from Allah سبحانه وتعالى.

91. Burn Yourself

As Salik drives to work each day, it was common for him to get cut off by rude drivers. This morning, a red sports car quickly pulled up to his right side and slipped to his front, forcing him to abruptly hit the brakes. Before Salik could note the offending car's license plate number, it had already sped off. Salik lost his temper, screamed and cursed, while slamming his fists on the steering wheel. In his rage, he accidently struck his cup of coffee off its cupholder, spilling hot coffee onto his lap. The hot liquid burned, but he had no one to blame. He had burned himself.

In practice...

Regardless of what others do to us, our reaction(s) or lack thereof is always in our control. We shouldn't blame others when we fail to control our actions or emotions. Usually, these outbursts of emotion when we respond to peoples' infractions often hurt us more than anyone else.

92. My Dependents

Abdul Rahman saw a mother and her son. The little boy was crying for a candy wrap at the cash register. His mother was adamant and told him he had already eaten enough sweets for the week. The boy would not let up and kept wailing. In compassion to the boy's distress, his mother capitulated and placed the candy wrap in her shopping cart along with the rest of the other items. Abdul Rahman prayed for the same type of mercy from his own Sustainer and Caretaker.

In practice…

It is appropriate for us to cry unto Allah سبحانه وتعالى for all our needs. Moreover, Allah سبحانه وتعالى is more merciful to us than our own mothers.

93.   Lord, Please Help Me

There was a man who was often seen in the mosque during the daily prayers. He constantly shared his problems and life challenges with the resident Imam. He would complain about his family members and other community members, claiming everyone was unjust to him. Perhaps, he used to do indulge in these to make him feel better. It never did. One day, the imam told him a harsh reality. He said: "Perhaps, you are stuck in difficulty, because you are in the real Helper's house and you have failed to talk to Him."

In practice…

There are circumstances where it is praiseworthy to seek advice. However, it is important to remember that other humans are not in the best position to solve our problems. In fact, their lack of sincere concern about our challenges can add more to our sufferings. The real Helper is Allah سبحانه وتعالى. Although others may not be is interested in our plight, Allah سبحانه وتعالى always prepares a way out for those who sincerely call on Him.

94.   Natural Disposition

As they walked towards the mosque, Adil and Adam were being followed by one of the neighborhood dogs. It followed them at a safe distance, barking defensively. Adil became very annoyed until Adam gently reminded him: "It is just behaving according to its nature." Once they arrived the mosque, Adil smiled and said: "Now, let's act according to our own nature." Then, they briskly walked into the mosque for their prayers.

In practice…

It is the (genuine) human nature[2] to establish a relationship with Allah سبحانه وتعالى. As a human being disobeys his Lord, he moves further away from this default nature. Then, the unnatural becomes natural, and humans begin to adopt behaviors and attitudes that are not in their best interest.

---

[2] This is called *fitrah*.

95. Pouring Mercy

Yousra sat outside crying. She was in a state of extreme difficulty. The specific details are not important. She was simply in hardship and seemed to have no way out. As she sat there, supplicating in her heart for relief, she felt water strike her head. It was a splash of rain. She couldn't help but adorn a smile. The rainfall was a glad tiding.

In practice...

Rain is a metaphor for relief in the Islamic tradition. Also, according to the statement of the Prophet Muhammad (ﷺ), *duas* are readily accepted during rainfall.

96.   Savor each Bite

Shakirah's first bite was good. She felt grateful for the food. Her second bite was better. She pondered that she had never been tested with hunger. On her third bite, she wondered how food in the afterlife must taste like. On her fourth bite, she contemplated what it must be like to dine with the Prophet Muhammad (ﷺ). It felt good to be a believer.

In practice…

Heedlessness is one of the most blameworthy conditions to experience. Muslims use every situation of theirs to remind themselves of the blessings of Allah سبحانه وتعالى and the afterlife that is quickly approaching.

97.   Evil Eye

Warda loved to invite her friends over to her home to show off her beautiful garden. Each day, she would have a new group of people in the garden, and she would explain the botanical origin of each flowers and how best to care for them. She couldn't help but notice that after a few weeks, her Tulips started to wilt. This was despite all her hard work in caring for the flowers. Warda decided to stop inviting people to "feast their eyes" on her garden.

In practice...

The prophetic traditions warned us against the evil eye. If we are astonished or like something (especially what belongs to others), we are encouraged to say, *"MashaAllah"* to ward off the effects of the evil eye. In the story, several people came to Warda's house and some of them probably liked the tulips. Perhaps, they didn't say, *"MashaAllah"*, and the tulips were affected by the evil eye, causing them to wilt.

98. Responsibilities over Rights

Shahid and Samirah were waiting in Dr. Siddiqui's office for their counseling session. They had marital issues and hoped the visit would help solve them. As they sat waiting for the therapist, they saw two sheets of paper that were left for them. Shahid picked up the sheet titled, "Rights of the Husband" and his wife picked up the other sheet titled, "Rights of the Wife". Suddenly, Dr. Siddiqui walked in smiling. He looked at the sheets in their hands and made the couple exchange their sheets with one another. "Lesson 1: Worry about your responsibilities and not your rights," stated Dr. Siddiqui in a formal tone.

In practice...

By focusing on your responsibilities, you give yourself some semblance of control in a relationship. It is a waste of time to solely focus on your rights when it is someone else's responsibility to fulfill them. More importantly, it is also against the *Sunnah* of Prophet Muhammad (ﷺ).

99. Last Bite

Salah's favorite food has always been Fried Chicken. Any time he had a chance to eat the crispy goodness was a time well spent. Today, he was devouring a huge plate of deep-fried chicken wings in his home with his friends, Wazir and Abdul Aziz. As they sat eating and chatting, Abdul Aziz reminded his friends about a class after *Isha* prayers and suggested that they all attend. They only had about 40 minutes to be punctual for the class. "What is the class about?", asked Salah, as he gobbled yet another chicken wing. "Spiritual growth and how to attain it," replied Abdul Aziz. Salah lifted his hand off the plate and said, "I think I have had enough."

In practice...

The Prophet Muhammad (ﷺ) said, "No human ever filled a vessel worse than the stomach. Sufficient for any son of Adam are some morsels to keep his back straight." A full stomach can serve as an obstacle to spiritual growth. Hence, a gradual reduction of food intake is part of the journey towards self-reformation.

100. Spoiled Appetite

Shah sat down at the counter and ordered a plate of waffles with scrambled eggs. As the young man behind the counter was preparing the meal, he was having a discussion with a co-worker about a mutual friend. They mostly spoke ill of their friend and mentioned several things about him that annoyed them. After preparing the meal, Shah was asked if he preferred a "dine-in" or a "take-out". He opted for the latter. As soon as Shah received his food, he left the store and turned the corner. Then, he threw the entire food into the nearest garbage can. For some reason, he was no longer hungry.

In practice...

The most important criteria for good food in the religion of Islam is that it is lawful and wholesome. However, there are some personal standards that are even higher than these. Some may not partake in a meal because they believe that a preparer's disposition or lack of spirituality in the person that cooked the food, may have an undesirable effect on the meal.

101. Get What You Asked For

Junaid's cat constantly attempts to go outdoors. One day, while it was raining relentlessly, Junaid tried to dissuade the cat from exiting through the cat door. Unfortunately, it kept evading him and continued trying to leave the house. Eventually, Junaid relented and let it go. A few moments later, with a sorrowful demeanor, the feline was back but totally drenched in water. Junaid reflected on his own state and asked Allah سبحانه وتعالى for forgiveness.

In practice...

Sometimes, we may desire what is harmful to us. Allah سبحانه وتعالى may not grant our desires or wishes because they are not in our best interest. But if we insist in trusting our own judgment over our Lord's, then we might eventually get what we desire. Similarly, the cat in the story insisted on something that its owner knew wasn't of benefit to it. Eventually it came back when it realized the reality of the situation. When we acknowledge our mistakes or misdeeds, the mercy of Allah سبحانه وتعالى is always near and available.

102. Late Night Openings

Abdul Qadir had a lot of issues to sort out. He lay on his bed late at night trying to sort them out. He felt stuck mentally and spiritually. After some reflections, he realized he was simply wasting his time and energy. There was a set time for solving these types of issues. He set an alarm for right before *Fajr* prayer. Then he went off to bed.

In practice…

The last third of the night is specified in Prophetic teachings as the ideal time for a servant to converse with his Lord. Problems that cannot be solved with our own strength and ability can be dealt with at this special time.

103. Grateful for the Small Things

Taha woke up in the morning and took a long and hard look at his right arm. He praised his Creator for every part of the arm from the shoulder to the fingertips. He thought about everything he would be doing with his arms throughout the day - brushing his teeth, lifting his spoon to eat breakfast, opening the door to leave his house, turning the steering wheel of his car, etc. It was a beautiful day to be alive. He looked at the top of his dresser – therein laid remnants of his orthopedic cast the doctor removed the previous day, a memory of his two months with a broken arm. The hardship was over, and life was good.

In practice…

Sometimes, a person may expect extraordinary things in life in order to be thankful to his Sustainer. However, after hardships or deprivation, it is somewhat easier to appreciate the small things. As Taha had just broken his arm, he found it much easier to be grateful for all that he could do with it.

104. Sincere Counsel

Saad sat patiently in the waiting room for his son's doctor appointment. On the other hand, his son, Abdullah, was not patient at all. The 9-year-old was running throughout the waiting room, pulling out magazines from the racks, and worst of all, disturbing others in the waiting room. Saad gestured for him to sit down but Abdullah refused to listen. His father realized that he would have to explain in detail how and why his son's behavior was inappropriate. Unfortunately, he would have to wait until later to do so. If he wanted his advice to have any effect, he would have to do it in private.

In practice...

It is very important not to hurt peoples' feelings when correcting or advising them. It is less important to focus on what we say, but more important to focus on how we say it. This means we should speak gently and must be considerate when offering counsel.

105. Signs in the Mundane

Dr. Kamran was walking on the seashore with his friend. While enjoying their walk, they saw a wood log in the sea, floating smoothly on the sea's surface. Dr. Kamran asked his friend, "Why do you think this log doesn't sink?" His friend replied, "Because wood is a less dense material than water." Then, Dr. Kamran responded, "Actually, the wood log does not sink because it does not panic." His friend smiled.

In practice...

There are always external (obvious) and internal (hidden) meanings to every little detail of life. In the story, although the wood log was very heavy, it did not sink. Dr. Kamran pointed to a deeper lesson behind the mundane explanation. The scene could allude to the idea of staying calm in the face of hardships.

106. Seek Knowledge

It was late Friday night and Qasim was exhausted. He had missed the weekly Friday night gathering in the mosque. There was no power on his phone, so he was also unable to listen to his daily admonishment lectures. Overall, it was a "spiritually dry" day. Right before he fell asleep, he grabbed his *Hadith* book off the bookshelf and opened a random page. He read the first *Hadith* he saw. The Messenger of Allah (ﷺ) said, "He who follows a path in quest of knowledge, Allah سبحانه وتعالى will make the path of *Jannah* easy to him." Qasim felt a sense of satisfaction and fell fast asleep.

In practice...

Islam mandates knowledge seeking for all Muslims. Fortunately, even little strides towards seeking knowledge each day qualifies you as being on the path of knowledge. Qasim understood this premise and tried to read one *Hadith* before the end of his day. This regular act helps him to maintain his status as a seeker of knowledge.

107. Veils Lifted with Age

This weekend was full of family drama at Grandpa Asim's house - one cousin offended another, an uncle had an altercation with his son, a nephew was having issues with his spouse's friends, etc. These issues (and more) were the topics of discussion as the whole family sat in the living room to review the details. That is, the whole family except Grandpa Asim. He simply sat there in his rocking chair, completely unfazed by all the issues. While the others spoke amongst themselves, he was seen mouthing different invocations as he clicked away at his prayer beads, one by one. He had seen it all, and like himself, it was all starting to get old.

In practice...

As a believer advances in age, he(she) starts to see worldly incidents for what they are. The same disputes and concerns repeat themselves, generation after generation. Once this is realized, one should turn his (her) attention to the only One that matters.

108. What Goes Around Comes Around

When upset, Murad used to yell at his daughter, and he would not allow her to explain herself. One day, Murad picked her up from school and again started yelling at her under the pretext of giving her advice. While driving home, out of nowhere, a car pulled up beside him. A man rolled down his side window, yelled at Murad and criticized his driving skills. Once the man drove off, Murad turned to his daughter and apologized. He had learned his lesson.

In practice…

As humans, everything that happens to us has (a) reason(s). Nothing is random. We should remember that in our limited human life, everything we experience presents an opportunity to improve ourselves and to ultimately, cultivate a better the relationship with Allah سبحانه وتعالى.

109. Cry of the Oppressed

It had been a whole week since the scary incident, but Hala was still visibly shaken. Afterall, she was robbed of all her valuables at gunpoint! She could have raised an alarm, but she was just too scared. Moreover, she had her infant son and toddler daughter with her during the confrontation, and she didn't want them to get hurt. Now in the safety of her home, she raises her hands in desperation. She knows that her cries would not go unheard.

In practice…

In several sayings of Prophet Muhammad, it is said that Allah is with those whose hearts are broken and those who are oppressed. The Prophet says, "Stay away from the prayer of the oppressed against you." In other words, if an oppressed person makes a prayer against another person (especially the perpetrator), there is no hindrance to the acceptance of that prayer.[3]

---

[3] This is also one of the sayings of the Prophet.

110. Rights of the Body

This Ramadan was intense for Irshad. He slept late, woke up early and was fasting for over 15 hours each day. He did these in order to maximize the benefits of the holy month. During the week, he spent the day at work, and the evenings and nights at the mosque. After the first two weeks, he really started to feel burdened by this routine. He woke up one Saturday morning feeling totally fatigued. He turned off his alarm and went back to sleep. He had wronged his body and it was now time to make amends.

In practice…

Islamic spirituality entails taming the desires of the body through some degree of self-denial. However, the body has rights and it is important to fulfill them. Ignoring these rights will eventually harm us.

111. Art of Discourse

Naseem's wife was telling him everything she disliked about his behavior and attitude. As she spoke, he couldn't help but notice the mistakes that she had made in her critiques of him. She had failed to acknowledge the good things that he had done for her and exaggerated all his shortcomings. However, he stayed quiet. Countering his wife's submission wasn't worth their conjugal bliss.

In practice...

It is an art to not be drawn into arguments. It is very important to avoid unnecessary confrontations at all costs. It helps to recognize others' disturbances and spiritual states before engaging with them. In the story, Naseem was spiritually skilled enough to consider the possible evil outcome of faulting his wife's opinions.

Glossary

Adab: good manners, especially in the relationship with God

Adhan: the Muslim call to prayer

Affair: relationship

Alhamdulillah: a chanted divine phrase of appreciation of God or Allah

Allah: proper Name of God in Islam

Allude: explain, refer

Anger: uncontrolled and chaotic human spiritual state

Appreciate: thank

Arabic: a language, especially the language of revelation of the Quran

Arrogance: feelings and actions of superiority

Assert: claim

Astagfirullah: a divine phrase of asking forgiveness from God and cleansing the heart

Behavior: the way one acts or conducts oneself, especially toward others

Bismillah: a divine phrase of starting anything with the blessing of God

Bowing: bending one's body, especially the act of respect by bending one's body, for God

Certainty: knowing without doubt

Chanting: repeating, especially in Sufism, repeating the phrases with focus and experience

Compassion: loving and caring

Conscience: internal instinct of distinguishing between right and wrong

Consciousness: awareness

Constant: not changing, permanent, especially in practice, known as Reflective Attributes of God

Death: end of physical faculties of a person

Discharge: negative states of spirituality that makes the person sad, stressed and anxious

Divine: transcendent

Dream: visions when one is sleeping or awake

Dua: supplications to the Creator

Ego: self, identifier of a person, especially in Sufism, raw and uneducated identifier and controller of a person

Ethical: moral

Ethnographic: based on observation

Etiquette: good manners and respect, respect in the relationship with God and others

Evil eye: the belief of unknown effects of the human eye across different cultures, traditions and religions, especially due to extreme hatred, jealousy or even excessive veneration

Evil: anything that causes stress, sadness or anxiety

Expand: enlarge

Fajr: (Salah al- Fajr or Salah al- Subhi) the Muslim daily prayer observed at dawn. Regarded as the first of the five daily prayers.

Fitrah: state of purity Muslims believe all humans are born with.

Genuine: sincere, original, authentic.

Hadith: Sayings, deeds, practices and silent approvals of Prophet Muhammad ﷺ.

Heaven: (Jannah) a place of all maximized pleasures of bodily and spiritual engagements in the afterlife

Hell: a place of punishment in the afterlife

Humbleness: behavior of modesty in viewing oneself, accepting the weakness in one's relationship with God and not being disrespectful and arrogant to God

Humility: character or trait of humbleness

InshaAllah: God willing, hopefully

Intention: planning ideas before the action

Isha salah: the Muslim daily prayer observed at night. Regarded as the last of the five daily prayers.

Islam: name of a religion that emphasizes belief in one God; and acknowledges Jesus, Moses, Muhammad, etc. as human prophets of the Creator

Itikahf: islamic practice of seclusion in the mosque for devotion, usually during the month of Ramadan.

Journey: struggles of following guidelines of a mystical school

Lord: God

MashaAllah: God has willed it

Memorization: learning by heart

Mercy: compassion and forgiveness

Mind: logic, reason and rationality

Miracle: incidents that defy the law of physics and other natural sciences

Mosque: house of worship for Muslims

Muhammad: the last Prophet in Islam

Notion: concept, idea

Oppression: unjust action of the strong over the weak

Pious: devout, practicing

Pronunciation: correct sounds of letters in a language

Prostration: the act of respect and submission to the Creator by placing the face on the ground.

Quran: sacred text of Muslims, the major source of Islamic jurisprudence

Recitation: reading

Reverence: respect

Reward: prize, payment, especially in world and the afterlife

Salah: prayer

Scent: perfume, nice smell

Scholar: expert who practice what they teach (alim)

Scripture: sacred book or sacred text

Self: ego, identifier of a person

Service: ethical action of doing good for others and society

Struggle: efforts to achieve a goal

Sufi: follower of Sufism

Sufism: mystical path of Islam

Sunnah: customs and practices of Prophet Muhammad ﷺ.

Temptation: false ideas

The Divine: God

Trait: permanent character or nature

Tranquility: peace and calmness

Transcendent: beyond human limits

Umrah: (Lesser Pilgrimage) islamic pilgrimage to the holy sites that can be undertaken anytime of the year.

Unseen: anything the five human sense organs cannot perceive

Weak: not having a physical strength to perform an action

Worshipper: a person who regularly follows and practices rituals and other acts of worship

Wudhu: (Ablution) islamic purification of cleansing parts of the body, usually in preparation for salah (prayers).

Index

www.ingramcontent.com/pod-product-compliance
Lightning Source LLC
Chambersburg PA
CBHW032136040426
42449CB00005B/270